The BUTTERFLY process

From Brokenness to Boldness

PORTIA BRYANT

BLUEPRINT PRESS INTERNATIONALE

ISBN
978-1-961117-48-8 (Paperback)
978-1-961117-49-5 (eBook)

THE BUTTERFLY PROCESS

From Brokenness to Boldness

About the Author

Portia Bryant is a multidimensional business professional, humanitarian, and author who has dedicated her life to helping others find their way through life's most challenging moments. With her extensive background in spiritual and emotional healing, performance, and community advocacy, Portia has helped thousands of individuals free themselves from emotional distress, achieve abundant living, and lead fulfilling lives.

As an empowerment speaker, music artist, and host, Portia has inspired and empowered countless individuals through her wise guidance on navigating life's obstacles with strength and resilience. She has provided Destiny Fulfillment Coaching and other programming to youth and adults alike.

In the face of the COVID-19 pandemic, Portia has continued to make a difference and was afforded the opportunity to expand her reach internationally, by branding online programs and curriculums. Almost 2 years following, she was invited to teach on the topics of Emotional Stability and The Ultimate Emotions Navigation System in Cameroon, Africa.

It is in her role as an author and performing artist (Absolute) that Portia truly shines. Her book and life guide containing all of the lyrics to her album, accompanied with practical rewarding and interventions, The Butterfly Process: From Brokenness to Boldness, speaks powerfully to the transformative process of emerging from trials and challenges as a stronger, more resilient version of oneself. With her signature blend of spiritual and emotional wisdom, Portia guides readers through the often-painful journey of healing, growth, and self-discovery, helping them emerge with a newfound sense of purpose, confidence, and joy.

As an international speaker, innovator, performing artist, coach, and qualified mental health provider with over 20 years of experience, Portia is a true powerhouse of inspiration and empowerment. Her passion for creating counseling programs, facilitating impactful group sessions, and offering engaging development presentations is matched only by her unwavering dedication to helping individuals unlock their full potential and soar to new heights.

Portia Bryant is a licensed minister, graduate of Old Dominion University & Averett University. She holds a Bachelor's degree in Human Services/Counseling and a Master's degree in Business Administration (MBA). She is a wife of 21 years and mother of two beautiful children.

Connect with Portia: portiabryant.com
                info@portiabryant.com

Dedications

*This book is dedicated to Grandma, Mommy,
and my beautiful sisters, Alicia & Chloe.*

*Grandma, my rock, you continue to fight the good fight of faith. Thank you for your model of unwavering
devotion to God.
I strive to carry out your legacy of holiness.*

*Mommy, you have taught me how to sing, smile, and enjoy the simplicities of life. Thank you for your
model of what it
means to truly be born again.*

Alicia, you taught me how to dream. I admire you for your ambition and fortitude in the face of all odds.

You are a true success story. I admire your ability to achieve.

I believe in you.

*Chloe, you are brilliant and beautiful in so many ways. I am enjoying seeing how resilient you are. I see
you blossoming
into a new place of prosperity continually. Thank you for not giving
up on the process. You are a diamond. Shine.*

*And to my daughter, Peyton, Goddaughter, Kori,
Nieces; Ravyn, Areli, Skylar, cousins; Brianna, Nia and Naomi embrace the process
you were created to blossom.
To my brother Brock, nephew, Rymahd, and cousins Able and Niles,
preparation plus opportunity equals success.
Remember to enjoy your journey and learn from each moment along the way.
Each of your lives speaks of a beautiful testimony of God's love and favor on our family.*

*Popz, Nez, James, Chi, Smiley, Jazz, Mya,
nieces, nephews, Uncle Glen and everyone connected.*

Thank you for you.

Acknowledgements

To God, my Father, You are the air I breathe. I appreciate You for all You are - all you have done, and all that you continue to do. Thank You for Your patience with me throughout the process of my spiritual development and pitstops. Thank You for never giving up on me. Your continued direction, favor and provision never cease to amaze me. I know that I have been unknowledgeable about resting in your peace because of my anxiousness to see the complete layout of my life, but I thank you for teaching me to slow down and appreciate life and each step as you give it to me. You have given me peace of mind to know that practicing and taking one step at a time makes all the difference. And God said, "How about you choose one thing and be faithful in that." Thank you Father.

To my husband, Charles Bryant, you have been there with me for over 10 years. It has been with you that I have learned to understand the process of receiving and giving the great dimension of agape love. I have learned that if I am to truly progress, I must get over...myself; invaluable revelation to progressing in the process. Thank you for joining me in my life's journey.

To my father, John Williams, thank you for being there and showing me your joy in the midst of the parenting process. Your hard work and diligence to seeing a vision come to past has truly inspired me.

To Bonnie, Rachel, Uncle Eldred, Pastor Davis, & Ma Kim, I appreciate your mentorship.

To LaKia, my spiritual nurse, India, Tamico, Adrienne, J-Chill and Makina you have been my confidants and you've kept me grounded and real throughout my process. To Uncle Earl, Brian Bean, Russ Johnson, Margo Taylor, Denise Long, Lady Branham, "MT P," Ronnie Ratliff, Karina, Aunt Alyce, Blessing, Helen, Dina, Armaggedon, Rosean, Donyata, Kiki and so many of my friends in the gospel and church family who have been there through various seasons of my life; I am forever grateful. Each of you has helped in the process to make me better. Much love to my brilliant mentee, La'Shay Lucas, I see you blossomin'!

To Archie "Vanzetti" Boone, the best God-Brother a sister could ever have. CATASH, brethren! Thank you for all you do. James Copeland, Shawn Dubose & Joe Hunt as well. I am forever grateful for all your contributions on the "Absolute Defines the Process" CD project. To Anthony Tillahun, you have been both a true friend and ace. Thank you for believing in me.

To Center of Hope, Oakland, CA, Grace Community Church, Fredericksburg, VA, Mt. Pleasant Baptist Church, Norfolk, VA, CVC Ministries, Women of Life, Norfolk, VA, HRCO, Churches In One Accord, and Women Connect, Portsmouth, VA; thank you for believing in me. Tabernacle of Deliverance, Chesapeake, VA, blessings, love & honor to the Apostles. I humbly respect & appreciate your commitment to being sensitive to the Holy Spirit in each service. Thank you for prioritizing the

Holy Spirit above 'agenda' in your services. Thank you to First Lady & Pastor Pete Carter for your belief and support of this project.

A special acknowledgement goes to Crosby Bonner & Rose Bonner, pastors of my home church who understood the mandate of discipleship; Love International Church, formally known as Alexandria Christian Center forever in my heart.

Love, admiration & respect to Pastor Richardson & Lady Richardson and all of my church family at Little Grove Baptist Church, Suffolk, Virginia.

Inspiration to create this workbook was inspired by a young man by the name of Courtney Josiah Franklin, Thank you! Children are indeed a heritage of the Lord.

TABLE OF CONTENTS

TABLE OF CONTENTS AND OVERVIEW OF CONTENTS

This workbook includes song lyrics, activities and discussions designed to help you embrace and progress, one step at a time.

LIVING EPISTLES

Be the change you want to see in others. Allow your life's "letter" to speak for you and encourage someone else.

BUTTERFLY

Discover who you are and admire yourself as God's beautiful creation. Be patient to transform and inspire others to do the same. "I see you blossomin".

MY TESTIMONY

Life is good, but many times we allow our negative emotions to blind the sight of our blessings. Work through your past, speak your process, live today, and help someone else to overcome.

PROUD VS. INVINCIBLE

Success and confidence without acknowledging God is a breeding ground for pride. Pride comes right before the fall. God resists the proud but gives grace to the humble. The first step to change is first to be honest and admit.

TEARS OF A HEART

No one ever said that life was going to be perfect. God wants to hear your struggles and concerns. Stay in a place of accountability. The more you reveal the better you feel. The less you conceal, the quicker you can heal. Use your tears and honesty to purge, and purify your heart. Then ask, "What can I change?"

REPRESENT

We go through life living and learning through experiences. We learn how to live our lives based on the values we adapt through what we see, hear, and participate in. Are you ready to give an account for what you represent?

HE MENTIONED ME

You are valuable; even while you were yet a sinner, Christ gave His life for you. Relationship and fellowship with God will allow you to recognize truth. In turn, understanding truth opens the door for your identity to be revealed. It is here where your value and self-worth is established.

TALK TO GOD

Mentally, spiritually, and emotionally, talking to God is an essential part of healthy living. Having a conversation with God requires honesty, an open mind, and an open heart. If you are willing to go to God, He is willing to receive you. Clarity, vision, and peace of mind await you.

CLOSE

In the presence of God is the safest place you will ever be. Allow worship to become a part of your lifestyle. No height nor depth, nor anything else in all creation, will ever be able to separate you from the love of God. The only thing that can do that is you. God is an all powerful ruler of the universe. Embrace His love for you. Do what it takes to get to know Him and become as close as possible.

STRAIGHT UP

Life is not perfect and we are imperfect beings. There are going to be moments when we are going to feel discouraged, but no matter what happens, we have to place God first. Spending time with God is an essential part of going through the process. God has a way of helping us when we feel there is no hope. Try spending time with Him and see.

SALVATION

Salvation is not something that can be bought or earned. Salvation is a gift from God. It is up to us to receive it. God knows all about you and loves you just the same. Surrender all by placing the responsibility of your life in His hands. Once you've developed a steady relationship with God, you have the luxury of watching Him do the rest.

PROCESS DEFINED

There are so many things that we have to face continually in different seasons of our lives. God takes us through quality control and checkpoints to see if we are ready for that next step. Embrace the process and it will prepare you. Preparation plus opportunity equals success.

AFTER THOUGHTS

After you've done all you can, it's time for you to reflect on where God has brought you from. Maturing in the process allows us to know when to slow down, when to be still, when to move forward, and when to ask for help. Live on purpose for purpose.

LIVING EPISTLES / ABSOLUTE

FEATURING VANZETTI

We are the epistles manifested in Jesus
Open it up and read us
Livin' la vida Jesus
People they need Jesus
Leaders they need Jesus
Nations I see them coming
They comin' runnin' for Jesus

Oh man to your city, to your city we come
See when we're playing in the game
Throw in your towel it's done
VA many cities
And the state where I'm from
VA, DC, Represent where you're from

Oh man to your city to your city we come
If I lose faith? No I won't be rapping, I'm done.
Jesus where that city where that city you from?
Christ said, "Oh my people you should know where
I'm from" Jerusalem? No man you loosing them.
Nazareth! Jesus Christ from Nazareth! Child be
blessed whatever the nation you're from you are
blessed. I'm doing my best, I'm walking through
the process and tests. It's me He met. I'm walking
even after my death! See that's a bold statement.
Gotta let you know statement. See that's a bold
statement knees hit the floor statement. Process of
going through, let Him guide you to.

Ok to your city, to your city we come
See when we're catching all the fame
Travel boarders like Pun
VA many cities
And the state where I'm from
VA, DC, Represent where you're from.

What's next?
I'm rocking' to the beat cuz I'm blessed
I trusted God and now I'm listening
And passing my tests
Bible text?
That's too much words to be reading

I don't know I do it anyway
I need it for breathing
Process, need it, breathe it, eat it, I'm sure
Pain and hurt? He's teaching a sista how to endure.
And I need you to walk with me, need you to talk
with me, reach to the stars with me, Come on you's
a star 'Bee'. Lean wit it, rock with it, smile it, dance
wit it, love wit it, hug wit it, That's what's up! You
can Lean wit it, rock with it, smile wit it, dance wit
it, love wit it, hug wit it, That's what's up! See!

Stand tall tell your city, tell your city march on.
See when we're catching all the fame
Travel boarders like Pun
VA many cities
And the state where I'm from
VA, DC, Represent where you're from.

Master plan! Take it to the Co-los-si-ans.
Freedom man, never stop taking a stand.
Get hype and dance.
"That's Christian music"
And I'm like AND???
Never stop representing
He walks with me,
Walks with me holding my hand
Now I see,
He smiled and He mentioned me
Talk God, Interlude, My Testimony
I define spoken word that's giving to me
Tears of a heart, now I see more "clearly" Aviator,
Navigator, you can get it now or later, Christ the
bomb picture painter, spread life because I'm able.
Real life, don't be a faker, let Him pot and remake
you. Sign off no need of staying I'll get back with
you later Holla! Yeah! Whoo! Uh!

We are to strive to live as an example for others to turn to Christ. Continue in genuine relationship with the Father. When mistakes are made, seek God, repent, and share your epistle with someone else.

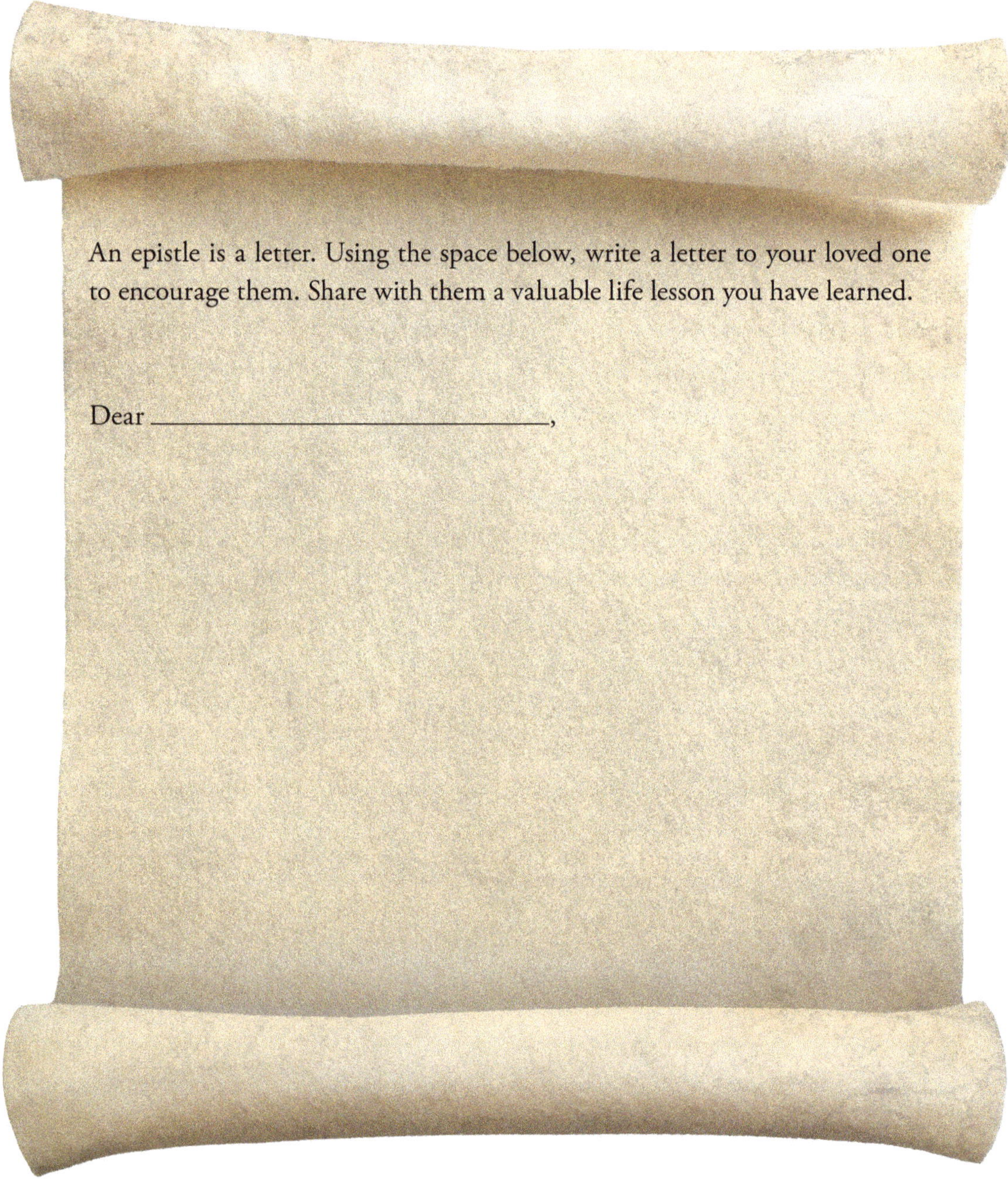

Group Discussion Question:
What would you say in a letter to encourage yourself?

Personal Challenge:
List 10-12 special memories from your lifetime. Writing section located on pages 54 to 59.

BUTTERFLY / ABSOLUTE

Butterfly. Huh?
He's... What?
They Way, the Truth, and the Life.
Yeah
(repeat)

Just call me lyricologist
Got beats to make you pump your fist
Words to make you stop and listen
Don't call me coward
Got words to make you shower
He's your power and your dream
To make you blossom grow up like a flower
Beautiful, butterfly make you high in the spirit,
make you cry in the spirit,
Don't you die in the spirit but the flesh
Make you grow up huh?
Change your mess, must confess, to be blessed
Super-fly, Butterfly, He's the way
Won't you try, don't deny...
Judas Priest; you must believe
Your heart is harder than Ali the fighter
For real, stop my friend and grab a piece of heaven
be free, yeah whooo, uh…

I come back on the beat to express to be free, Jesus is your only need, look at me I'm on my knees, pick you up you in my hand help you dusting off the sand, His command, my child you have to crawl before you stand, Butterfly cocoon, He's making room for you gain the land, the process is to make you humble man. Focus on the glory not the middle of the story, giving honor to The One who's due,

What? Read the Bible try to catch a clue, huh? Spiritually we're learning how to walk. Fill me with your Spirit Lord teach me how to talk. What's the cause? We can't be patient. I know it's not so easy but it's worth it. Dreams and visions are like a baby waiting so birth it yeah, whooo, uh…

Butterfly I see you blossomin so beautiful the colors. Angels they rejoice, I see you made it through they wonder. Your life is like a Bible it's a story give Him glory. Tell them all about it. What? Ministry is real; helping heal the hearts because they shed so many tears. Wonderful, gentle, majestic; See you're butterfly! Jesus is the air everywhere now see you better fly. What? Breathe hope. What? Breathe peace. Show them with your life that He's the only one they need. And see the multitude bowing at the knee. He's supreme, the King, making hearts sing, breathing peace. Yeah Whooo Uh!

Yeah eee yeah alright ight ight ight alright yeah whooo.
I see you blossomin'(3x) Yeah
I see you blossomin'
I see you blossomin so beautiful the colors, angels they rejoice I see you make it through they wonder.

BUTTERFLY / ABSOLUTE

Blossomin' is not allowing anything to stand between you and your relationship with God. It is reaching an all around new level of success and prosperity.

The song "Butterfly" is about sharing the gospel in a way that informs and welcomes others to a relationship with Christ by offering a word of encouragement and seeing them as God sees them. This activity will teach you some of the ways God sees you as well.

DIRECTIONS: God really does love you. Look up scriptures listed below, make each scripture personal using "me" or "I" in your paraphrase. Turn to pages 13 and 14 to write what each speaks to you the most. Read over your responses, highlight key words and include them in the butterfly image shown below:

Ephesians 1:4,5
1 John 1:9
Romans 8:28
Romans 5:1
Ephesians 2:10
John 3:16
1 John 3:7
1 Peter 2:9
Colossians 3:12
Psalms 139:13-14
Jeremiah 29:11
Romans 5:8
Matthew 5:14
Psalms 139: 1-3
1 Samuel 16:7

Discussion:
What was your favorite scripture? Why?

____

Challenge:
Using your highlighted keywords and favorite scriptures, write an affirmation statement using the following format: I am... I know... I believe... I will... Therefore...

____
____
____
____
____

Example Scripture to look-up: 1 John 3:7

1 John 3:7 says, *"Little children let no one deceive you whoever practices righteousness is righteous, as He is."*

Writing Example: God expects me to try.

Ephesians 1:4,5

---

1 John 1:9

Romans 8:28

Romans 5:1

Ephesians 2:10

John 3:16

---

1 John 3:7

---

1 Peter 2:9

Example Scripture to look up: John 3:16

John 3:16 says, *"For God so loved the world that He gave His one and only Son, that whoever believes in Him shall not perish but have eternal life."*

Writing Example: God really loves me.

Colossians 3:12

____

____

Psalms 139:13-14

____

____

Jeremiah 29:11

____

____

Romans 5:8

____

____

Matthew 5:14

____

____

Psalms 139: 1-3

____

____

1 Samuel 16:7

____

____

Life goes on people change, nothing ever stays the same.
Don't give up if you try, gotta keep your head to the sky.

Father's house, brothers, sisters, didn't see them no more. Mother loved us, did her best, couldn't take the detour. Then I found the One that abounds, age 4 and some more. The Lord kept me and He really had His hand on me. Devil tried to take me. What? Tried to destroy me. See boys touched, what in the world I was only a kid. Many times tried to question what it was I did. Moved to grandma's Forest Edge babysitter won't good. Older sister went to school couldn't save me from this. Age 4 still touched couldn't take it no more. 5 years old kindergarten, better than it was before. Grandma had us going to church. On the weekdays too. No pants, all skirts, many people did dirt. Seeing grandma pray. Always stayed on us every day. Cooking meals, providing clothes, momma called every day, getting herself back together, back at home, it was cool. I had an uncle, dude, I remember praying for you.

Jesus came to visit one revival morning, it's true. Ashland me and my sister visit summer glory like Whooo! Exposed to some of the things the Lord would have me to do. Singing, reading, preaching gospel, blocking out worldly views. Age 6, Lord was teaching, pulled me close to His heart. Couldn't tell you why. But I never wanted to part. Seeing grandma when she prayed. Soaked in tears when she wept. Court thing, went to mother's, back at home it was best. 7 years old had an uncle that I looked up to, went to college after high school, very smart dude. Strong man, to the family, he was like the glue, a year later found cancer, now he's gone and I'm blue. He had a baby named Brianna years less than 2. Now I'm sad and I'm mad. Maybe he'll be back soon. Age 11, nurtured years with my dad he's cool. Took us out for some rides, bike and movie or two. Went to church down the street, Jesus planted my feet. In the midst of it all, He came and rescued me.

ASSIGNMENTS:

Age 12, 13, accept Him as Lord of my heart. Young girl read the Bible, kept me away from the strife. Without it, self discovery, the world just ain't right. A lot of stuff was going on. My sister running away. Middle school flew by. High school on the way. Opened environments of some of the things I mentally chose. Good God was there. What? He kept me up on my toes. I was involved in the church youth ministry. Was accepted by the pastor meant so much to me. Youth revival, Brownsville, new perception it's true. Taught me all about rejection, how it's used as a tool, to get you off the course that was really meant for you. Seeds planted young age, curiosity, meditated, wrong things, lustful thoughts I see. Met my husband 10th grade, we were sweet hearts yeah. But rejection came to haunt me, sexually active again. Repented to the Lord over and over again. Now this was something that I really need Him teach me to stand. Momma couldn't take the disrespect I gave. 17 moved away, back to Grandma's again.

Self sufficient drove a car had a job and all. Grandma helped me to transition to the college not far. Away from hometown, university life won't for me. High school sweethearts got married 18. Had my struggles through them years. Nah it wasn't a breeze; college, tuition, jobs, marriage, and my family. Years later, what do you know, minister in Fredericksburg. The husband and I walked with God, kept Him close by our sides. "Live in Norfolk," Lord said. "Walk by faith" and I try.

As I look back on all the hurtful things I been through: insecurity, rejection, inappropriately touched. When I was young. I was a witness of way too much. But through it all Lord Jesus understands me. Anything could have happened. Could be dead spiritually. Full of joy, more mature and I got my degree. Stay focused Lord said, "Draw closer to Me." Yeah.

If we don't deal with issues in our past, they will continue to control us in some way in our present. But they don't have to. We can deal with past sin, our family histories, as well as past violations to our bodies and minds.

1. Write a letter to the person who has **hurt** you the most.

2. Write a letter in response to your letter from their **perspective**.

3. Write a letter of **forgiveness** to release yourself from burden.

Definitions & Group Discussion:

See Glossary for definitions.

Testimony: ____

Hurt: ____

Perspective: ____

Forgiveness: ____

Declaration to begin...

My Testimony is that I have a testimony. I have a story that others can relate to. I feel hurt, I feel pain, I feel happy, I feel sad, and I feel joy. I am able to see the perspectives of others. I am able to both apologize and forgive. Today I am a new person; I am allowing myself to be in a position where I can start living beyond my hurt feelings and past circumstances.

Pride has no place in me. I accept peace and forgiveness. Today I walk in confidence and boldness through the Spirit of Christ. What the enemy meant to destroy me, God can turn it around for my good.

Challenge:

Write a letter of apology to someone that you have wronged. (Share the letter with them) The letters found on the following pages are optional to be shared. Many find it liberating to write, be honest, and finally be given a voice to express themselves.

Write a letter to the person or situation in life that has hurt you the most.

____
____
____
____
____
____
____
____
____
____
____
____
____
____
____
____
____
____
____
____
____
____
____
____
____
____

Write a letter in response to your letter from their perspective: (If you chose to write about a situation that has hurt you the most, try looking at it from another perspective. Start your writing with: "On the other hand..."

Write a letter of forgiveness to release yourself from burden and/or write a letter of acceptance and growth.

Let me talk to you for a moment. See you know I have problems too. An awkward place to start off, but I'll say it cuz it's the first thing on my heart. See I had and have some maturing to do. Went my whole life thinking I knew so much, only to discover I had no clue. But now I know that with life comes lessons to be learned those end results of tests taken, failed and passed has an impact on your life that will last. After repentance, God's grace and forgiveness, deeds that have been done cannot be erased.

When sin is done it plants a seed so deep. It starts to grow you pray and weep. I used to think that God's commandments and rules of holiness were just there for us to know and if I broke a moral law, all I would have to do is repent and the sin would go. Now I don't know if I thought that after repentance the sin would somehow transcend and vanish. But I know now where it goes and where it grows and where it's planted. I know now why I can't take God's grace for granted.

God has rules and commandments, not for His convenience, but for our protection. But many times because of our hurt, pain, curiosity, feelings of rejection, feeling like nothing less than. We choose to participate in the very actions that negate Jesus dying on the cross and taking away the pain. To every action there is a reaction. In the mental, physical and spiritual realm; inevitably, not only do we have to face God but we have to face ourselves. Day in and day out you'll be reminded that you did everything you thought you were big and bad enough to do. Not realizing how much those very things could destroy you.

Now I know why God is the way He is. Our Father, want to protect us from those things that we claim to see but don't. Walking around thinking, "I'm the Invincible One." But now I know that this is a proud and prideful attitude. Lord look at me now, I'm humble, ready to subimit...to You.

"If my people which are called by my name will cry out, humble themselves and pray, I will heal..." **(2 Chronicles 7:14)**

What is something you know about yourself but you don't like to admit?

____

____

____

____

____

____

____

Definitions:

Pride: ____

Invincible: ____________________________________

Humble: _______________________________________

List 3 phrases from page 21 that caught your eye or would help you if you applied them to your life.

1. ____

2. ____

3. ____

Small Group Discussion Questions:

What are the dangers of pride in your life? What are the benefits of being humble?

____

TEARS OF A HEART / ABSOLUTE

FEATURING VANZETTI & CATASH

What's up world, peace, peace, what you cryin for. yeah, I understand…why, Jesus. Christ! Love you, it's still the process the logic doesn't make sense but keep your head up. I'm Vanzetti the narrator, what's up! And I got Catash on my side. Absolute! Listen here's the story.

Man I'm strugglin', money hustlin', bill jugglin', need that hundred end. Sellin' cds, album eps, for a small fee, price of coffee. Man I'm off see, four mouths to feed, one on the way, wanna run away put the gun away, what my son a say, man it's such a life, wanna clutch the knife, end it all today, simply fall away, I'm hoping yall will pray, cause I got dolls to raise, take my car & keys, cuz my heart bleeds, and it's hard to breathe, took a part of me to give you all of me, no pops to father me, chastised by the wise, avoid the robbery, perhaps the lock and key, still it's hard to see, how we gonna eat, hole is getting deep, bills are overdue, clouds they smoulder you, so what's a soldier do? Man I don't have a clue. - Catash

So why do we cry, why ask why, why do we try, why do we die, why, it's a hope on the other side, we gone ride through, I'ma take you over here to the back woods, welcome home, over hear, VA beach each one teach one, Norfolk city, 757 I got somebody, who comes from a higher realm, a realm of the knowing…Absolute! Welcome home.

Man I'm strugglin', know it's common man, Jesus let me in, wanna be your friend, know it's out of sight, let Him be my might, mappin out the plight, journey and a fight, no one understands, no they not my friend, doin' all I can, must I take a stand judge me not and know, with the pain I grow, no it's not a show, this is me I'm bold, unlike I've been told, it's all about my soul,

Life's incredible, it's all about the goal, Jesus take my hand, I need you now I know, now I got to see, to be more for thee, give my soul to thee, give my all to He, body carryin', flesh is marryin', dirty things again, comin' to an end, on the Word I stand, wanna understand. Lord I wanna understand.

They still don't understand though, it's a process step by step, kinda works like a cycle, c'mon, I see your feet still movin, you got knocked off the bike but a, get back up (put your pads on), c'mon, uhh, get em up, wipe that man off, listen, wipe that girl off, shoulders high, chin uptime, show her some love, time, Absolute last one.

Open bible now, time to take a vow, promise and a vow, letting out a shout, what it's all about? Love without a doubt, realign my route, no more sit and pout, affirm the things I know, that I gotta go, get up out of here, Christ is carryin', to another realm, cuz my heart is felt, and it's me He kept, when my spirit left, oh today He dealt, on my knees I knelt, I give my all to Him, wanna be with Him, cuz it's best for me, when I walk and see, cuz I'm able man, time to take a stand, Jesus sent the few, what am I to do, give my all to Him, and I'm counselin, in my Spirit chair, in my soulful prayer, why am I so scared? I need you Lord I'm here.

(so look into my eyes) so don't forget (see the tears I cry) talk to God (look into my eyes) let Him know (why they askin' why?) where you stand at wit Him right now (we rise) confess your sins (from the bottom) Romans 10 verse 9 (to the top we flow) give your life, give Him your time (let's go we flow) it's His anyway (let's go) I appreciate it Catash (Talk wit Him) Absolute. I'm Vanzetti the narrator, Keep your head up.

Discussion: Do you think boys should be discouraged from crying? What are the purpose of tears? What about the song is most memorable to you and why?

____

What are (5) things that you struggle with? List five challenges that block your overall success in life.

1. ____

2. ____

3. ____

4. ____

5. ____

Definitions: Using the glossary, read the definitions of each word listed below. Next, write a sentence using the word. Be sure to make the sentence personal by using "I" in your statement.

Repent: ____

Serene: ____

Courage: ____

Accept: ____

Group Challenge:

Repeat the following prayer together -

"God grant me the serenity to accept the things I can't change, the courage to change the things I can, and the wisdom to know the difference."

On the following page write something in your life that matches the underlined words:

*"God grant me the serenity to accept the **things I can't change**, the courage to change the **things I can** and the wisdom to know the difference"*

*"Tears can sometimes be the necessary rain
for the blossoming of our souls." - Absolute*

Group Discussion:

What are some examples of things we cannot change in life?
What are some examples of things in life we can change?

Complete the following LIFE chart:

Things I am concerned about that are on my mind most often...

____
____
____
____
____
____

Things I can't change...   **Things I can change...**

_________________________	_________________________
_________________________	_________________________
_________________________	_________________________
_________________________	_________________________
_________________________	_________________________
_________________________	_________________________
_________________________	_________________________
_________________________	_________________________
_________________________	_________________________
_________________________	_________________________
_________________________	_________________________
_________________________	_________________________

Group activity:

Share your LIFE chart. Pray the *Serenity Prayer* for one another.

REPRESENT / ABSOLUTE

Beat too hot to represent the wordly nation. Smile with me now, Absolute the one who claiming. (3x)

Clickety Clack/I'm coming to flow on the mic on this track/I'm scared to go back/God helped me put my life back on track/Rickety tat/I'm trying to give you something you can feel/Not missing the ills/I'm trying to seek THE TRUTH/And it's real/I'm born again/Accept the call disciple I am/" Ilie call my friend/In the midst of the storm I will stand/I'm not backing down/I'm living this life for God pound for pound/went round the town/I spoke to God in Christ I was found/I'm Absolute/Praise and worship is what I do/I flow and it's real/The Word of God can penetrate through steel/This is my story/I flow to you to give God the glory/I'm praising Him now/On judgment day to Him I will bow.

Rit tat here we coming/where my peoples is at? Baseball many innings/ Now you up at the bat/ Much love to the fans man/they up in the stands/

Speed it up/ keep it going man they clapping their hands/Holy Spirit speak THE TRUTH/Man you know what to do/ You seen their eyes tearing?/Pick em up...Tie up their shoe/Watch the people getting wit it/I'm hip and ready "to spit it"/ our lives...it's time to give it...the message is in the building.

Beat too hot to represent the wordly nation. Smile wit me now, Absolute the one who claiming (3x)

12 Bars wasn't really only time I was given, sit back take notes, now it's time to listen, beat rocks hot ready burning up in the booth. Holy Spirit main Man, Jesus adequate proof, yeah. Ah ha hah hah diddy diddy daddie day. Jesus wont you take my hands and wash my sinful nature away, hey. Ah ha hah hah hah diddy diddy daddie day. Jesus is the only One. He's THE TRUTH and THE WAY. Hey. Do you really understand? Do you really understand? Huh what? Do you really understand huh what? Do you really understand? Do you really understand, huh what? Get ready, get ready, get ready for The Process now.

What do you represent?

Look up the following scriptures then create personal daily affirmation statements by summing up the verses and using "I" statements:

CLEAR CONSCIENCE - AFFIRMATION

Romans 8:1

____

____

____

LIFE & PEACE - AFFIRMATION

Romans 8:6

____

____

____

HELP WITH WEAKNESS - AFFIRMATION

Romans 8:26

____

____

____

PURPOSE - AFFIRMATION

Romans 8:28

____

____

____

CONFIDENCE - AFFIRMATION

Romans 8:31

SECURITY - AFFIRMATION

Romans 8:39

POWER & STRENGTH - AFFIRMATION

Philippians 4:13

FULFILLMENT - AFFIRMATION

Philippians 4:19

FREEDOM - AFFIRMATION

John 8:32, 36

Receive your benefits as a child of God.

What do you represent?

Write a script for a commercial making Christianity appealing to the masses.

What do you represent?

Imagine that during an interview you are asked to answer the following question:
Why did you choose Christianity? Or why do you think that someone should consider becoming a Christian?

Ah huh what's up we back again, He mentions me and calls me friend. Ah huh what's up we back again, Absolute come through and rap for them.

It's incredible, Jesus Christ, what, so unforgettable, so let it go, pain, His love so unconditional, 3-Dimensional, bi-optics, two-tops my optics, who fought this, yeah. It's undeniable, common sense ink, pad and what pencil, the physical, yielding my flesh what to the spiritual. Hear me flow, full course my vocab you hear me speaking, Vanzetti MC God's friend believe it. Absolute flowin' breathe stretch release, she living right. Rocking more than Jesus pieces, hear me pleases. Fro and Wunda Fam release, who the Son sets free yep is free indeed, you got to keep re-pen-ting constantly to live believe, looking back on Adam and Eve. Bible is the Truth so evidentially, to my Father yes He prayed and He mentioned me, what?

It's undeniable Agape love sent from above, look at the dove Holy Spirit holds and hugs, look at me, What, I'm dying to the flesh, that's what's up, I'm praying on my knees and saying, "Can you fill up my cup?" Jesus please, healing all my wounds with ease, giving up your life discover that you gotta take heed. Search and seize all the stuff that lives in me, pray and breathe for open opportunity.

Smile and see that Jesus is the one for me, lock and load; to please Him is the ultimate goal. Winning souls, warning sent so now you've been told, I volunteer my life avoiding all the wicked and strife, I dedicate my life I tell you I'm "a praying for wife." Hyper C, the husband, it is he who she like, the Word is strong like a bond eat it, take a big bite. Making wrong decisions? Then I'll have to read you your rights.

He mentioned me. John 17:20, tried for me, sighed for me, died for me. Finally, freedom glory on the day 3, take a seat devil, take a peep, read it and weep, take and believe it, you lifting hands up high to receive it, One Supreme it, on His knees He prayed for me and, dying to flesh, counselin' with the man, Ca'tash.

Give it your best, tell it to the world, then you rest. I'm better off since I read it, I said it, so don't forget it. Prayer, what, peace, and healing, in Christ you're so appealing. Accept? Reject? Tell me when they willing to let, Him into their souls, come on people stand and be bold, the time has come, Father let your will be done. He prayed that we keep it safe, pure and holy and true, what? Tell the people that it's time to choose. In the Garden, where? Jesus in Gethsemane. Now He walks with the Father for eternity. Whaat?

How do you see yourself? Pause for a moment to think about it.

What thoughts have you had about yourself this year?

____
____
____
____
____

Many of us find ourselves:

- basing our self-worth on how others see us and on our accomplishments
- feeling shame from our past
- defining our value based on our looks
- setting unrealistic standards for ourselves

But it doesn't have to be this way.

If only we could see ourselves as God sees us!

John 17:20 - Jesus thought enough to pray for you while He was on his way to be crucified. He said, *"I pray not only for the disciples but also for all who will ever believe in me."* God sees you at your full value.

Answer the following questions:

Value Statements: "I am important" "My life has meaning"

1. What makes you feel like you are not valued? I do *not feel valued when...*

____
____
____
____

2. What makes you feel valued? *I feel valued when.*

____
____
____
____

Answer and discuss:

Which illustration is worth more?

A.   B.   C.

    A. Perfect

    B. Balled up

    C. Stepped on

    D. All of the above. No image has lost it's value.

In spite of the brokenness and abuse we have experienced, we still have to see our value as not being diminished. We are not defined by our past experiences. We can choose to break free.

When Jesus was on His was to Calvary, He stopped in the Garden of Gethsemane and prayed for us. Take a moment to write a prayer.

Remember the A.C.T.S. acronym to help you with your prayer = **Acknowledgement** (Give 'props' to God for all He is; tell Him how much you adore Him), **Confession** (apologize/repent for any wrong doings and/or those things that you have allowed to stand in the way of having an even closer relationship with Him), **Thanksgiving** (What are you grateful for?), **Supplications** (requests) - What do you want God to do for you?

A =

____

____

____

____

C =

____

____

____

____

T =

____

____

____

____

S =

____

____

____

____

Discussion:

God knows all about you and loves you just the same. What would God say in a prayer for you?

____

TALK TO GOD / ABSOLUTE

Talk to God yeah, Talk to God yeah, Talk to God yeah, Talk to God, Talk to God

I met a lady by the name of Mary, sister of Lazarus. I heard her spirit speaking to Jesus. Who? Of Nazareth. She said, "I worshipped you, adored you, paid my dues, told you all about my problems, you just took it as news. I gave my all to you, witnessed, and I prayed for souls. Now you out of town by choice when I need you most. See my issues I gave you with confidence see. I believed that you would come through. You were sent for me. The very action that I asked you, be faithful, prevent. Was the very issue and I'm sick and so sad it happened. Now you're here days later, I'm still running to you. You tell me that you love me and you haven't forgot. And you want me to remember that it's You that I got??? How can I, when you left me hanging emotionally. How can I trust you when my heart feels emptiness see. How can I trust you?"

Then Jesus stepped by her side with tears swelled in His eyes, and said, "My child the hurt I feel I can't decide. Haven't I always been there for you inevitably? Now you're here at my feet crying doubtin' on me? Pain is something that we need to go through in life.

God helps me and He'll help you to get through the strife. Without pain we can't grow. Look at me cuz I know. When pain is managed by the spirit in productive ways. Our character grows, our life shows, our hearts obey.

I'll tell you what to do, just keep believing in me. Be faithful, press on, cuz I'm guiding your feet. Can't you see me now steadily here and guiding you see?"

"I'm sorry Lord Jesus, you're right, I'm wrong, now I see that pain is here just to help me be strong.

Reflection on my past says you're bringing me through, and now I see I was wrong for ever doubting in you."

"It's cool," said Christ, "You're called for purpose and life. This will work out for your good. Walk by faith not by sight."

Dear Lord, It's Absolute, I need to speak to you. Sometimes the hurt is real can you guide me through. I can't do this by myself I need your strength to get through. Footprints in the sand tell me what to do.

God glory! Strength cuz I made it through. I clench my fist and grit my teeth but I made it through, and uh Jesus help me come upon a new view and Lord, extend your peace for the rain and blues.

What!!! I get distracted so easily. Spiritual attention deficit woe is me. And uh hurt is real, sin is thicker it's true but when I talk to God I see that He's bringing me through. "It's cool said Christ. You're called for purpose and life. This will work out for your good. Walk by faith not by site."

Part of the process of life is being able to "Talk to God" in the good times as well as the bad. God knows you. Take the time to be honest with Him as well as yourself. Increase in knowledge, understanding and wisdom.

Through Communication - Prayer

that was easy

Group Activity: Form 2 circles: One circle of people on the inside and one circle of people on the outside. Face one another. Practice the simplicity of prayer by praying about something that comes to mind. Rotate right and switch partners when prompted to do so.

Discussion: 1. Discuss a list of 4-6 top things you can pray about every day. 2. See if you can locate the purpose of pain in the Talk to God lyrics on p. 36.

Challenge: Pick something in your life that you have found difficult to deal with on a daily basis.

Use the lines below to record your daily challenge. Check off and record your results in the journal located in the back of this book. While praying, practice something positive concerning your challenge. *If you continue to do what you've always done, you'll always get what you've always got.*

____

____

____

Pray about it for 7 days straight.

Monday ___ Tuesday ___ Wednesday ___ Thursday ___ Friday ___ Saturday ___ Sunday ___

Attention: When you have completed this 7 day challenge, think about more personal difficulties to purposefully pray about on a daily basis. Record your thoughts and prayers. Complete one challenge at a time; Life is a journey, not a race.

Note: Stay committed and seek God's guidance for as long as you are disciplined to do so.

When we practice talking to God and bringing Him into our everyday lives, we begin to see His relevance and feel His presence.

We can talk to God about anything, anywhere and anytime. What comes to mind, right now, that you would like to say to God? Use the speech bubble below to write your conversation.

You

Prayer is a 2-way conversation.
Don't forget to listen during your devotion time with God.

God

Don't miss hearing the voice of God.
1 Kings 19:11-12

Lyrics: *"Walking through the process can sometimes be a lonely place. When you get discouraged, close your eyes, and know, that He's so close...He is... So close." (Worship & Meditation track)*

We get closer to God by worshipping Him. Worship is an act of offering our souls to God (Soul = Mind, will, and emotions). When our attitudes, behaviors, thoughts, and bodies are used for the purposes of God, we are in a safe place. The safest place to be is in the will of God.

*How much time do you spend looking at your cell phone every day? Most people spend at least two hours a day. Add God to your daily routine by downloading an **interactive** daily devotional application on your cell phone.*

Discussion:

Being Christ-like... What does that look like?

____

Are people really able to be Christians and remain close to God in today's society?

____

____

____

What was/is your Behavior, Intervention, Response, & Plan (B.I.R.P. note) for getting Closer with God?

____

____

____

Write your **BIRP** note

Behavior - How have you observed your emotions & behaviors to be?

Intervention - Recently, what helpful principles and strategies have you been exposed to that will help you to become a better version of yourself?

Response - How have you responded to the new knowledge you gained?

Plan - How do you plan to implement your own success strategies moving forward?

What are some things you can do every day to remain close to God? Be sure to give supporting details for each of your answers.

1.

____
____
____
____

2.

____
____
____
____

3.

____
____
____
____

4.

____
____
____
____

Instead of wondering, "How close to 'the world' can I be and still be okay?" We should be asking, ***"How close to God can I be?"*** Don't settle for being attracted to things of this world, but rather pursue holiness with all that you are.

God wants to use you to display His glory to a world that desperately needs to be impacted by the reality of Jesus Christ. Sometimes we allow things and people to get in the way of our relationship with Jesus Christ.

2 Corinthians 6:17 (NKJV)

"Therefore come out from among them and be separate," says the Lord. "Do not touch what is unclean, and I will receive you."

Don't give the enemy anything to hold over your head. Escape baggage, weight, guilt, and shame by practicing becoming closer to God. Truth be told, there are some things we have to walk away from in order for this to happen.

Find the definition of "fasting" on page 51 and write it on the lines below:

Fasting:

____

____

____

Personal challenge and discussion: Try fasting to experience peace. With your character in mind, illustrate and label in the space provided below "weeds" in your life that you want to eliminate and "flowers" you want to grow.

If I read my Bible and go without ____

____

__________________________for ________ days, I would be closer to God.

STRAIGHT UP / ABSOLUTE

Lyrics: *I know we get caught up sometimes, but we have to remember that while we are going through the process, we are not perfect, and in spite of... "Dot... dot... dot" we have to place God first. And in doing that, never, shall we ever, lose our... salvation...salvation...salvation.*

Discussion:

Quote from Billy Graham (a globally respected Christian leader)...

"The Christian life is not a constant high. I have my moments of deep discouragement. I have to go to God in prayer with tears in my eyes, and say, 'O God, forgive me,' or 'Help me.'"

Everyone has things in their lives from their past, or present, that they aren't particularly proud of:

- You may have had somthing happen to you that you have not told anyone, or perhaps only a few people.

- Perhaps you feel shame about certain aspects of the family you grew up in.

- Maybe you have sinful habits which you feel embarrassed about, such as impure thoughts, gossiping, lying, lusting, pornography or criticizing others.

- Maybe you have done things in your past you are ashamed of such as an abortion, lying, stealing, or hurting someone.

- Or maybe something has been done to you that you feel ashamed of (i.e. sexual assault, emotional abuse).

"The more you reveal, the better you feel...the less you conceal, the quicker you can heal" - Unknown

Where in the Bible can we find the scriptures listed below? Write the answers on the lines provided.

ALL have *sinned and displeased God at some time.* _______________________________

There is no condemnation for those who are in Christ Jesus. _______________________________

We have a standard to live by..Be ye holy for I am holy. _______________________________

He who practices righteousness is righteous. _______________________________

Discussion: Waiting to exhale...
What happens when secrets are kept?

Challenge: Seek God for wisdom.
Don't be held captive by a secret.

hile processing through life, don't forget to live.
*is came that we might have **life** in abundance.*

I PLEDGE 7-MINUTES EVERY MORNING

"In the morning You hear my voice, O Lord: In the morning I prepare a prayer for You, and watch and wait for You to speak to my heart." - Psalm 5:3

If this practice isn't a regular part of your life, a good way to start is to take just **7-minutes** to be alone with God. When we know and love God, and live in harmony with His purpose it produces tremendous benefits in our lives.

Worded from a personal voice, here is a little guide on how to spend 7-minutes with God. You may want to alter or increase your devotion as time goes on. This is designed to help you begin and/or strengthen your life practice of devotion.

Take your life back today...

Teach me your way, Oh Lord, and I will walk in your Truth. **Psalm 86:11**

1. I will take the first minute to prepare my heart and mind for this encounter with God. Be still & quiet. Breathe and relax. Think about who God is to you. Talk about anything that has been bothering you. Acknowledge areas where you have been wrong.

2. Then I will take 4-minutes for reading the Bible. Remember, God's Word is Him actually speaking. Just read a little bit and think on what you've read. Think how you can apply the verses to your thoughts and actions this day.

3. Now I have 2 minutes left to speak to God in prayer. Let this be spontaneous. Thank Him, praise Him, share your innermost thoughts with Him.

I will close the door, silence the phone, and make an appointment time with the Lord.

____

I understand that making a habit of spending even 7-minutes in the morning with God can change my life.

In the morning I will rise, go to a lonely place, and pray.

sign: ____ *date:* ____________________

SALVATION / ABSOLUTE

One, *trust God, together, we're working hard, three - The Holy Trinity, forever He is God. One, trust God, together, we're working hard, three - The Holy Trinity, forever He is God. One, trust God, together, we're working hard, three - The Holy Trinity, forever He is God.*

Thank God for salvation knee shall bow from every nation every patient that I'm facing fallen soldiers on the pavement, I preach the gospel lady so why we talking shady? I speak this honest truth regardless of your morning paper. We're sharing the covers with Ruben Stoddard and Nancy Reagan. They gave me one line but I'm fine who reads the paper? Look at these lower nations; I pray that families make it, all of your cousins, yo uncles, yo aunties, they related, been feeling heavy lately, but I been interceding believing will you save 'em? They needing Christ like hurricane relief lights. They won't sleep at night. Cuz governmental street fights, we saw these levies breech, right? They want the Bread of Life, the living water wit some ice, and I done seen the coldest nights Norfolk city sort of like. The City of refuge, man we sort of like, we need to get on the streets and preach through the mics. So get your blue mics, now get your two mics, this one's for new life, we praise God we do right, salvation, there's a congregation in there waiting, yes! Every tongue confess. Yes! Every knee shall bow. Wow check it out.

Thank God for Salvation, peeps shall walk from every nation, everyone that needs a blessing, one suggestion, don't be stressing.

Keep it coming like the ancient of days. Deep breath ministry spread life eternally, so I move to the left and I move to the right and I feel the Trinity 3 fold family healing you let it be age 3, memory, drugs and infidelity, the world needs ministry. Thank God for salvation African and all creation every nation don't be waiting, time is ticking, contemplating. But while we're here we're going to struggle, just let the Lord be you muscle, in everything I see the Gospel is the word I need. To all the many nations, all of us we face temptations, Tahiti, Guam and Asia Open arms let Him embrace you. We got the same excuse. Somehow we're victims got abused. Despite it tell it He's THE ONLY ONE decide and choose.

Thank God for salvation, listen to speculation, God is the picture painter and also the picture framer. Talking to get you thinking start walking now get ta praising, embark on newer places, sparking up this conversation. Vision is celebrated Genesis to Revelation, salvation, celebration, heaven is for all races. That's why we call nations, watchmen on the gate waitin. Stop faking let it loose, now strap on your boots. If you ain't got none, take mine, I got some, if you ain't hot son hell is a hot one. They shot one down He fell to the ground and Satan and all of his demons they bowing to the ground, well my authorities, senority, supporting me, 3 cord embroidery we serving Him with loyalty, yes I'm in awe with God He is my royalty.

SALVATION / ABSOLUTE
FEATURING VANZETTI

Salvation is a gift from God. Using the circle below, use colors, shapes, symbols, words, and other images to create an image that represents who you are mentally, spiritually, and emotionally. Come as you are, surrender your life to the hands of God, and let Him do the rest.

Romans 10: 9, 10 - 9Because if you acknowledge and confess with your mouth that Jesus is Lord and in your heart believe (adhere to, trust in, and rely on the truth) that God raised Him from the dead, you will be saved. 10For with the heart a person believes (adheres to, trusts in, and relies on Christ) and so is justified (declared righteous, acceptable to God), and with the mouth he confesses (declares openly and speaks out freely his faith) and confirms his salvation.

PROCESS DEFINED / ABSOLUTE

In learning about life's journey, I discovered the process. And now I will attempt to break it down for both you and I to understand. The process is a series of changes we experience in our lives that are not completely painless.

The Process is...

When God gives us a path to choose and we proceed from one place to the next, not always knowing what's best.

The Process is.

God's method of stabilizing or conditioning us to move forward as part of a spiritual progression or character developmental state in our lives.

The Process is.

God's intention for us to submit to treatment in preparation to thinking, believing, and being the exact object of God's affection.

The Process is.

God's routine handling procedure in which He takes our lives through quality control and checkpoints.

The Process is.

Going through and learning how to submit our hearts to being analyzed thoroughly by God.

The Process is.

The ultimate experience, broken down into stages that we should take delicately one lesson at a time.

I'm Absolute-signing off,

Process Defined

Group discussion: Have you noticed any patterns that reoccur in your life?

____

____

____

____

```
A  F  J  J  H  J  G  E  Z  P  C  U  N  D  C
P  B  B  G  I  C  O  N  T  R  O  L  F  J  U
L  A  T  N  E  M  P  O  L  E  V  E  D  L  K
S  P  Z  I  C  H  E  C  K  P  O  I  N  T  S
U  E  M  Z  N  A  C  C  D  A  U  C  A  Y  P
B  E  L  I  E  V  I  N  G  R  H  N  T  E  I
M  T  E  L  I  T  L  H  I  A  W  U  S  N  R
I  U  S  I  R  I  Z  U  R  T  R  Z  R  R  I
T  L  S  B  E  Q  U  A  L  I  T  Y  E  U  T
M  O  O  A  P  J  C  D  H  O  Q  V  D  O  U
W  S  N  T  X  T  X  N  T  N  O  I  N  J  A
K  B  N  S  E  G  A  T  S  C  H  A  U  K  L
K  A  P  R  O  C  E  S  S  D  G  Q  I  V  H
S  S  Z  U  J  G  N  I  W  O  N  K  S  N  C
D  E  N  I  F  E  D  X  Q  H  H  Y  S  U  X
```

ABSOLUTE	CONTROL	EXPERIENCE	PREPARATION
BELIEVING	DEFINED	JOURNEY	PROCESS
CHARACTER	DEVELOPMENTAL	KNOWING	QUALITY
CHECKPOINTS	DISCOVER	LESSON	SPIRITUAL
UNDERSTAND	SUBMIT	STAGES	STABILIZING

Challenge: Part of boldness is being able to speak your testimony.

Using the word bank listed above, pick vocabulary words to share your life's process. 1. Write your testimony in the back of the book. 2. Using the vocabulary listed above, take turns speaking to the group about what you have learned during your process.

AFTER THOUGHTS / ABSOLUTE

(INTRO - Piano Plays)
Take me, in your arms, Fa-ther
I need you...to show me... The way
I can't go, I can't go, I can't go alone, oh no
I need, you with me, oh Lord
Make me strong, make me strong, make me
stron-ger Lord. make me Stron-ger

(Piano Plays)
Take me, mold me, shape me
Show me, the way, yeah

I can't go, I can't go, I can't go, a-lone
Without you, no no no no
Make me, stron-ger, oh Lord
I can't give up, I can't give up, oh no
With you I can, I can, I can make it
Oh Lord
Take me, shape me, mold me, change me
Into what, into what, in to what
You need..me to be. yeaaah.
Thank You..ooooh.
Process.

Directions: There is power in your words. Cast your vision. In the following activity, fill in the blanks using the word bank provided.

<table>
<tr><td></td><td>Living Epistles</td><td>Butterfly</td><td>My Testimony</td><td>Proud</td><td></td></tr>
<tr><td>Invincible</td><td>Tears of a Heart</td><td>He Mentioned Me</td><td>Represent</td><td>Talk to God</td><td>Close</td></tr>
<tr><td></td><td>Straight Up!</td><td>Salvation</td><td>Process</td><td>Defined</td><td>After Thoughts</td></tr>
</table>

People are looking at me to see if it is even possible to be a Christian. Ghandi said he would have been a Christian had he ever met one. My desire is to be an example of Christ's character and influence my friends to be _______________ for God's kingdom.

I understand that just like the _______________, I must go through a process to be matured to accomplish great things. _______________ is that I have a life story that will help others to become stronger, wiser and better. Therefore, I will let go of being _______________ so I can receive correction. I will put an end to feeling that I am _______________ in order for me to make better decisions for my life. I will cry my _______________ and remember that _______________ on His way to Calvary saying, "I pray not only for the disciples but I pray also for those who will believe" I am a believer! I am confident in who I am. For I know who I _______________.

In the good times and the bad times I will remember to _______________. I understand that in order to grow spiritually and get _______________ to God I will remember to study the Bible daily. _______________ Salvation is given by God through grace, not by anything we can ever do for ourselves. I thank God for my soul's _______________.

I remind myself everyday that "I can, of myself, do nothing" to earn salvation - my belief and confession of Christ's death, burial and resurrection has already taken care of that. It's already said and it's done. I know what I have to do; my _______________ has been _______________. All of my _______________ and meditations will be on whatever is true, whatever is noble, whatever is right, whatever is pure, whatever is lovely, whatever is admirable, excellent and praiseworthy. Christ's character of love, gentleness, self-control, patience, goodness, peace, faithfulness, kindness and joy are all showing in my attitude and behavior more and more every day.

Challenge: Once you have completed this activity, repeat the vision statement in sync as a group.
Group Discussion: (Journal Entry) Which devotional activity in the process impacted you the most? Why?

ABSOLUTE - perfect, whole and complete; lacking nothing.

ACCEPT - to understand, and/or receive what is being offered

AFTER THOUGHTS - to reflect on what has happened, what is, and what is to come.

BELIEVING - a faith and a certainty that something will come to pass; a whole heart's faith.

BLOSSOMING - the process of entering a new realm of success and prosperity.

BOLDNESS - a God given confidence that allows one to soar past their limitations; knowing who you are, and being comfortable in your own shoes.

BROKENNESS - 1. the process of being humbled so you can be in position to be taught; a place where pride cannot reside. 2. the feeling of being crushed, devastated and stuck in despair.

CHANGE - the process of acceptance and transformation; the process of what occurs after true repentance.

CHARACTER - who you are; the DNA that makes up your personality; your nature and values (I.e. kind, peaceful, selfish).

CHECKPOINTS - the places where you are evaluated and assessed for right standing; if one is willing, this in the place where you are refilled and equipped.

COURAGE - exercising boldness and confidence, while having a good spirit.

DEFINED - to be identified, taught and described with clarity.

DISCIPLESHIP - the process of teaching a new believer how to mature spiritually: devoted to God in word and deed (Disciple as one would teach a skill to an apprentice).

DEVELOPMENTAL - the expansion and increase of a state of being (i.e. character).

DISCOVER - the result of finding out something that you did not know before; to have a revelation and become aware.

EVANGELISM - to spread the "good news" by means of introducing others to Jesus Christ.

EXPERIENCE - the result of having obtained knowledge and skill through first hand exposure.

HEALING - the process of being cured; facilitating a remedy to recover from a traumatizing experience.

FASTING - to separate yourself from things that distract you from God; consecration.

FORGIVENESS - letting go of the need to be connected to an offense and the offender.

HUMBLE - freedom from pride and arrogance; recognizing that one's righteousness is "as filthy rags" in the sight of God.

HURT - to harm, wound, or damage.

INVINCIBLE - the feeling and belief that one is indestructible, indomitable, unbeatable.

JOURNEY - a figurative description describing life's experience as a voyage, trip, or passage to eternity.

KNOWING - having an absolute certainty; never doubting or assuming.

LESSON - a tutorial and/or hands on experience where knowledge is obtained and wisdom can be gained.

LIMITATIONS - Barriers and shortcomings that keeps you from blossoming.

PERSPECTIVE - the way a person, place, thing or idea is seen; a viewpoint.

PREPARATION - the process of getting ready for opportunity or advancement.

PRIDE - placing oneself in the position, place, or throne of God; a mindset that places oneself at the center of the universe; an inability to admit or change wrongful actions.

PROCESS - the stages of development where maturity and sustainability are obtained.

PROUD - the attitude of arrogance, conceit, and overconfidence.

QUALITY CONTROL - a necessary stage within the process that is designed to check one's alignment with purpose, excellence in character and management of emotion.

REPENT - to sorrowfully regret, and change one's mind and behaviors toward a person or God.

REPRESENT - what one stands for and characterizes; to stand before a people as an ambassador.

SALVATION - the gift of a soul being rescued and recovered by Jesus Christ to escape eternal disgrace.

SERENE - quiet; at rest; undisturbed; peaceful; not agitated.

STRAIGHT UP - to be real, honest, and open about topics that are considered taboo or difficult to discuss.

SPIRITUAL GROWTH - the process in which one's inner man has submitted to the process and developed resulting in allowing God's glory to shine.

STABILITY - the state in which one enters into a calm, soothing, and steady state of wellness; the result of one's life that is operating in balance.

STAGES - the phases and/or levels in life that one goes through to complete their development process.

SUBMIT - the ability to humble one's self to advance to the next phase of spiritual growth.

SUSTAINABILITY - the ability to maintain and uphold character and discipline.

TESTIMONY - the evidence, witness and demonstration of God's involvement in one's life.

Answer Key to exercise on page 50. People are looking at me to see if it is even possible to be a Christian. Ghandi said he would have been a Christian had he ever met one. My desire is to be an example of Christ's character and influence my friends to be **Living Epistles** for God's kingdom. I understand that just like the **Butterfly,** I must go through a process to be matured to accomplish great things. **My Testimony** is that I have a life story that will help others to become stronger, wiser and better. Therefore, I will let go of being **Proud** so I can receive correction. I will put an end to feeling that I am **Invincible** in order for me to make better decisions for my life. I will cry my **Tears of a Heart** and remember that **He Mentioned Me** on His way to Calvary saying, "I pray not only for the disciples but I pray also for those who will believe" I am a believer! I am confident in who I am. For I know who I **Represent**. In the good times and the bad times I will remember to **Talk to God**. I understand that in order to grow spiritually and get **Close** to God I will remember to study the Bible daily. **Straight Up!** Salvation is given by God through grace, not by anything we can ever do for ourselves. I thank God for my soul's **Salvation**. I remind myself everyday that "I can, of myself, do nothing" to earn salvation - my belief and confession of Christ's death, burial and resurrection has already taken care of that. It's already said and it's done. I know what I have to do; my **Process** has been **Defined**. All of my **After Thoughts** and meditations will be on whatever is true, whatever is noble, whatever is right, whatever is pure, whatever is lovely, whatever is admirable, excellent and praiseworthy. Christ's character of love, gentleness, self-control, patience, goodness, peace, faithfulness, kindness and joy are all showing in my attitude and behavior more and more every day.

12 Stages Of The Butterfly Process Check Off List

Each Representing a Frame of Mind

THE BUTTERFLY PROCESS OBJECTIVES:

STAGE 1 - LIVING EPISTLES

A mind that says, "I have something to give."

STAGE 2 - BUTTERFLY

A mind that knows what their Creator thinks of them.

STAGE 3 - MY TESTIMONY

A mind that has overcome a challenging life situation.

STAGE 4 - PROCESS VS INVINCIBLE

A mind that is able to admit areas of needed growth.

STAGE 5 - TEARS OF A HEART

A mind that knows what it can change and what it can not.

STAGE 6 - REPRESENT

A mind that knows its identity in Christ.

STAGE 7 - HE MENTIONED ME

A mind that knows it's value.

STAGE 8 - TALK TO GOD

A mind that understands the importance of conversing with its Creator.

STAGE 9 - CLOSE

A mind that is determined to never let go of God's hand.

STAGE 10 - STRAIGHT UP

A mind that recognizes that no one is perfect.

STAGE 11 - SALVATION

A mind that understands salvation is not earned but accepted.

STAGE 12 - PROCESS DEFINED

A mind that understands the meaning of life.

AFTER THOUGHTS

A mind that understands the purpose of reflection.

"Be ye transformed by the renewing of your mind." - **Romans 12:2**

Journal Pages

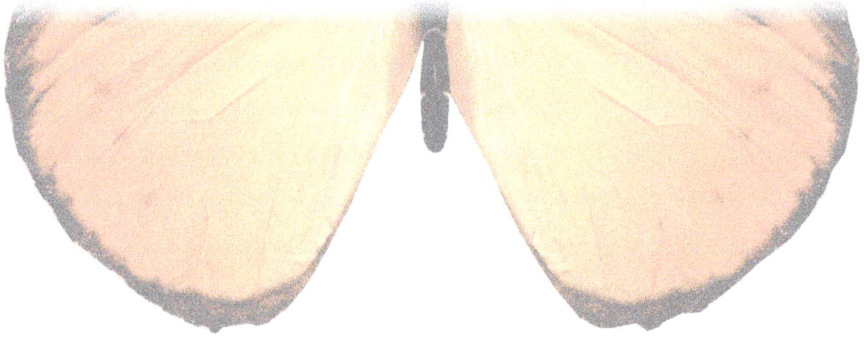

*Everyone that has been given the gift of life has to go through the process,
I prefer to do it with The One who created me. - Portia*

Scan the QR code
for the Companion
Music to access
the music links.

www.ingramcontent.com/pod-product-compliance
Lightning Source LLC
Chambersburg PA
CBHW041039050726
47599CB00018B/2023